THE SPIRIT OF DOOR COUNTY

A PHOTOGRAPHIC ESSAY

THE SPIRIT OF DOOR COUNTY

A PHOTOGRAPHIC ESSAY

Darryl R. Beers

Introduction by Tom Davis

Library of Congress Catalog Card Number: 98-61881
ISBN: 0-915024-68-3

The author and publisher gratefully acknowledge permission to excerpt quotations from interviews used for production of the audio tape, *Door County Tapestry*. Selected passages appear on the following pages: 16, 30, 33, 35, 38, 45, 47, 49, 50, 59, 71, 75, 76, 86, 101, 111, 115, 116, 121, 124.

Door County Tapestry © 1994 by
Trails & Tales
1860 Preble Ave.
Green Bay, WI 54302
(920) 437-0637

07 06 05 04 03 02 6 5 4 3

Editor: Stan Stoga
Designer: Nadine Paplow
Printed in China

Trails Books, a division of
Trails Media Group, Inc.
P.O. Box 317
Black Earth, WI 53515
(800) 236-8088
e-mail: info@wistrails.com
www.trailsbooks.com

PHOTOS ON PREVIOUS PAGES:
PAGE 1. CHERRY BLOSSOMS & CLOUDS, FORESTVILLE
PAGES 2 AND 3. DOOR BLUFF HEADLANDS, ON GREEN BAY
PAGE 3. SAILBOATS AT DUSK, EAGLE HARBOR, EPHRAIM

Dedication

To my Dad,
your unconditional love,
compassion and thirst for knowledge
continue to guide my journeys
and ease my burdens.

To my Daughter, Melissa,
for the countless joys
and wondrous meaning
you have added to my life…
for all that you have taught me.

HISTORIC LOG HOME, BAILEYS HARBOR

TANUM FOREST EVANGELICAL LUTHERAN CHURCH

Preface

How does one describe the essence of this small, unique Lake Michigan peninsula which we call Door County? Even the best of authors, with great command of our language, have, by their own admission, struggled to find the appropriate words which would answer this question.

Perhaps it is a matter of perspective—Door County is a lot of different things to a lot of different people.

For myself, the Door Peninsula has been a source of inspiration for my photography as well as a source of nourishment for my soul. I have seen the magic of its light, felt at peace with the calm of its waters, trembled at the force of these very same waters, drank in the beauty of its natural areas, smelled the fragrance of its blossoms, been drawn to the allurement of its villages and been absorbed by the vitality of its seasons. Whenever I have been blessed with the opportunity, I have sought to capture the essence of these experiences on film—with all the respect, integrity, passion and skill that I possess.

The photographs that follow are the result. They constitute my perspective of Door County—a perspective which I am grateful to be able to share with you, the reader.

Just as the character of the landscape which marks Door County is unique, so is the character of the people who live, work and play here. This is evidenced by the charm of its villages, the distinctive cultural features of its architecture, the attractiveness of its rural countryside, the diversity of its arts and richness of its history.

While many of these attributes can be captured on film, there remains an inner substance which demands a more in-depth approach to this human side of the Door County mystique. What better means to provide such insights than the people of Door County themselves—in their own words—expressing their feelings, revealing their thoughts, and recounting their stories. Interspersed throughout the book, these words give added meaning to the photographic images, incorporating the human spirit which is such a vital part of the Door County experience.

It is my intention that this book will serve to honor the traditions of the past, illustrate the beauty of the present and assist in creating a wise vision for the future. May the pages that follow stimulate your senses and lead you on a pleasurable journey through the special place known as Door County.

INTRODUCTION

THIS SLENDER SPIT OF STONE

By Tom Davis

What business I had in Fish Creek, I can't recall. My best guess is that I was meeting a friend for breakfast at the White Gull Inn, but I have no memory of the event. All I remember is what I saw that dewy summer morning, driving across from Baileys Harbor on County Highway F.

County F is a largely unremarkable road. Oh, it's scenic enough, in an understated way, winding through a pastoral landscape of dairy farms, orchards, and idle fields, a quilt of muted colors stitched together by solemn stone fences. Gangly sandhill cranes stalk these fields on stilt-like legs in spring and early summer; come autumn, the golden stubbles go black with clamorous Canada geese. There are a few landmarks: the Maple Grove Gallery, where Gloria Hardiman creates exquisite handwoven fashions in what was once a bustling rural grocery; the Greenwood Supper Club, which attracts a standing-room-only crowd of tourists and locals alike, night-in and night-out, for steaks, fresh whitefish, and prime rib. (Thankfully, backing for the golf course that would have disfigured the lovely cedar swamp between the Greenwood and Fish Creek seems to have fallen apart.) Nearer Baileys Harbor stands one of my favorite homes in all of Door County, a renovated, green-shuttered two-story farmhouse with a shiny metal roof, a roof that, especially on sharp-edged winter nights, reflects the moonlight like a beacon.

DAWN, ROCK ISLAND SHORE

Where F splits off from EE, it trends generally northward for perhaps ¾-mile bisecting the Gray family farm (the Holsteins are herded across it to pasture after the morning milking) before bending west. As you approach the curve, the road rises slightly; not much, but enough to afford a view of the low-lying basin that stretches out ahead.

That cool morning, fog had collected there, nuzzling into every fold and crevice, building to obscure the details of topography, the very braille by which we read a landscape. All that was visible were the crowns of the trees—maples, beech—in a few scattered woodlots, looming like mysterious islands in a misty, Arthurian sea.

I parked on the shoulder and stared in wonder. It was as if the earth itself had been transmogrified. I half-expected some mythical beast to materialize, a griffon, perhaps a unicorn, or that a dragon-prowed long ship would suddenly emerge from behind an island, its oars dashing the sea-foam in fury.

It was an accident of meteorology, of course; I suppose it could have happened anywhere. The point is, it didn't. It happened in Door County.

This happened too. We were camped on Rock Island—to my mind, the most enchanted address in Wisconsin—sitting around the fire in the afterglow of a perfect day. Rock Island lies two ferry trips from the mainland, but it is chiefly a journey of the imagination, a journey that cannot be measured in miles. There had been hiking on the green-canopied trails, sea kayaking (the water clear as desire) below the imposing cliffs, exploring the Great Hall built by Chester Thordarson when he dreamed of re-casting Rock Island into his personal Icelandic fiefdom. There had been swimming too, and the simple, indolent luxury of sunning on the island's one crescent of sand. We'd watched the squat tugs, gulls trailing behind like smoke, as they returned with their catch to Jackson Harbor, perhaps the last true fishing village on Lake Michigan.

Late in the afternoon, we'd assembled in the grassy clearing behind Potawatomi Light. Constructed in 1836, it's the oldest lighthouse in Wisconsin, and one of the ten that give Door County the historic distinction of more lighthouses than any other county in the United States. We'd brought cheap wine and expensive pate, plastic cups and paper plates, and we sprawled in the grass, drinking, eating, laughing. At the edge of the clearing, less than a hundred feet away, stood several apple trees, trees just beginning to drop their crimson-streaked fruit. "Look!" someone whispered. A pair of deer, young forkhorn bucks, had slipped from the shadowed forest for a meal of apples. They were unconcerned with our presence, and so close we could hear the apples crunching between their teeth.

But that moonless, cusp-of-autumn evening, the lake a black void dividing heaven and earth, we saw something that transfixed us. A galaxy of lights, a rogue nebula detached from its constellation, suddenly appeared in the distance. The sight struck us dumb. No sound accompanied it; there was just the crackling of the fire, and the eternal sibilance of the waves. It made the hair stand up on our arms. Finally, someone spoke: "It's a freighter." Somehow, this knowledge did nothing to lessen the spell.

This is Door County. It is also sunrises that boil out of Lake Michigan like lava, and sunsets that alchemize the sheer limestone bluffs into walls of solid gold. It is the spring sky-dance of the woodcock and the tremulous chorus of sandhill cranes; it is October's smoldering ribbons of color and enormous, pale-blue shards of ice heaved up on rocky shores as if the frozen bay were a lobe of an advancing glacier. It is solemn stone fences, fragrant fields of windrowed hay, and weathered-gray barns; it is trilliums covering the forest floor like soft new snow. It is history and culture, companionship and solitude, the good earth of memory and the imagination's point of departure.

But no matter how you add up the parts, the whole is always something more. There's the recreational angle, for example. I lived in Door County for nearly 14 years, and I discovered first-hand that the peninsula more than lives up to its billing as a gigantic playground—for adults. Bicycling, cross-country skiing, and flyfishing for smallmouth bass (all for which the Door is famed) were temptations I was rarely strong enough to refuse. Needless to say, my productivity suffered. In my defense, however, friends visiting from out-of-town marveled that I was able to accomplish *anything* in a place of such entrancing charm.

This brings up another factor in the Door County equation: the profound state of relaxation it invariably induces. The "why" of this has never been satisfactorily explained, although there's no doubt that the tonic effect of the water is a critical variable. For many people, the framework of a perfect Door County vacation comprises a cottage on the shore, a comfortable Adirondack chair, a couple of good books, and a libation or two with which to toast the sunset. A few days on the Door are guaranteed to reduce the fiercest type-A executive into a mellow, barefoot beachcomber.

In common with similar peninsulas, islands, and other enclaves considered remote by the rest of the world, Door County has long been a haven for artists, free-thinkers, and sundry square pegs who don't fit into the round holes of conventional society. I have this pet theory that there is a global centrifugal force, as yet undiscovered by science, that gradually separates the eccentrics from the normal run of humanity and spins them to the geographical fringes. While there's no denying the fact that Door County is becoming more gentrified, I like to think that there will always be a few colorful locals around, people like commercial fisherman-cum-actor Jeff Weborg, potato farmer/apple crate-maker/polka maven Freddy Kodanko, and contrarian man-of-letters Norbert Blei—not to mention assorted hyper-cynical bartenders and waitresses who sling a double order of attitude along with the hash. Life on the Door would be far duller without them.

Nearly two million tourists visit Door County every year—roughly the same number as visit the entire nation of New Zealand—and the figure is growing steadily. The danger is that tourism will mutate into an insatiable monster, a monster that threatens to devour the very qualities that make Door County unique. Some argue that it's already happened. There is much glib talk about "sustainability," about the need to balance economic growth with environmental protection and keep development on a scale commensurate with the dimensions of this slender, exquisitely fragile peninsula. But sustainability, in any form, implies limits—and no one in a position of influence (including county government) seems interested in imposing any. A savage greed is afoot in the land, and skyrocketing property values have only fanned its flames.

Which is not to say that a person doesn't have the right to make a decent living. In this regard, there is grave concern about the future of an industry that is virtually synonymous with Door County: cherry growing. The brutal bottom line is that the cost of producing a pound of cherries vastly exceeds the price that processors will pay. While pick-your-own operations remain profitable, there isn't sufficient volume to sustain more than a few token orchards. With developers offering top dollar for subdividable acreage, a land-rich, cash-poor cherry grower is in a tough position. No one, especially the orchardists themselves, wants Door County's fruit industry to survive only in memory.

There is, however, at least a partial solution to this vexing problem. Across the "Big Pond" on Michigan's Old Mission Peninsula, a traditional cherry-growing area experiencing the same kind of intense development pressure that Door County is under, voters recently put their money where their mouth is and passed a property tax increase designed not only to save the orchards, but to preserve the rural character of the landscape. The monies generated by the tax increase are earmarked for a fund that is tapped to purchase the development rights to local farms. These rights in turn, are held in trust by local government, which has the legal authority to intercede if and when development is attempted. It's a win-win situation: Orchardists get a financial shot in the arm, and everyone is able to enjoy the beauty of the blossoms, and the bounty of the earth.

Tendering a similar proposal in the townships of northern Door County has been discussed, but no action has yet been taken. The consensus seems to be that the political climate is not yet right. Given the fact that it may be the last best hope for preserving northern Door's rural essence—an essence rapidly eroding as more and more banal "country homes" are built—we can't afford to wait much longer.

In the meantime, groups like The Nature Conservancy, the Door County Land Trustees, and The Ridges Sanctuary continue to work, individually and in partnership, to protect the peninsula's special places. You've likely heard of the Mink River Estuary, the most biologically rich ecosystem of its kind on the entire Great Lakes. But you may not be aware of the Shivering Sands upland/wetland complex, the Kangaroo Lake Ecopreserve, the Porte des Morts Forest & Wildlife Preserve, or the Baileys Harbor Boreal Forest and Wetland. All are presently ongoing projects that will ultimately preserve thousands of acres of open space, scenic vistas, and critical habitat—habitat not just for familiar birds, plants, and animals, but for many rare, threatened, and endangered species.

The Door County Land Trustees, for example, recently purchased a site that supports Wisconsin's second-largest colony of Ram's-head Lady's-slipper orchids, an impossibly rare and delicate wildflower native to the upper Great Lakes. I'm a former member of the Door County Land Trustee's board of directors, and when the purchase was announced a member of the media asked me why we felt it was important to save this inconspicuous little plant. My reply—by no means an original observation—was something to the effect that all life is interconnected, and that to lose even one strand of the ecological web is ultimately to diminish ourselves.

But what I was really thinking is how unenlightened the question itself was. I'd thought that, as a society, we'd finally progressed past the frontier mentality that measures value solely in terms of tangible, quantifiable benefits. I thought that the question, "What *good* is it?" had been purged from the vernacular.

Just as Door County has been prodigiously blessed by nature, however, so too has it been blessed by visionary men and women—Jens Jensen, Emma Toft, Dr. Albert Fuller, to name a few—who never subscribed to such mercenary logic. The upshot is that few, if any, places in the upper Midwest have a prouder, stronger tradition of environmental stewardship. The incredible foresight that led to the establishment in 1910 of Peninsula State Park all but boggles the mind, as does the fervor and tenacity that, in 1937, resulted in the creation of the foremost wildflower preserve of its kind, The Ridges Sanctuary. Today, its sternly magnificent headlands and deep, unbroken forests make Peninsula the crown jewel of Wisconsin's state park system—just as The Ridges, its trove of rare plants rooted in what were Lake Michigan's ancient shorelines, is among the gems of the state's network of natural areas. Door County boasts 14 such areas, which protect unexploited plant and animal communities for the benefit of future generations. Toft's Point, where the fondly remembered "Miss Emma" ran her resort (several of the hand-hewn log cabins remain standing) is perhaps the best-known and most accessible; bald eagles nest in the towering pines, and the waters of Moonlight Bay, as flawlessly green as emerald, surge against the fissured ledgerock.

The limestone geology, the effects of glaciation, the micro-climate produced by proximity to Lake Michigan: These and other factors have combined to endow the Door Peninsula, this slender spit of stone, with a quotient of biodiversity—and scenic grandeur—out of all proportion to its size. From boreal forests to calcareous fens, from the most important whitefish spawning grounds in Lake Michigan to meadows that afford vital "rest stops" for migrating monarch butterflies, from the blossoming orchards to the sparkling bays, Door County's natural wealth is staggering.

With wealth, however, comes responsibility. Protecting the Door's remaining unspoiled places—protecting its *essence*—is not up to "them." It is up to *us*.

Tom Davis was a Door County resident for 14 years. For the last three of those years, he served as the Executive Director of the Door County Land Trustees. A Senior Editor for Wisconsin Trails *magazine and a widely published freelance writer with several books to his credit, Davis now makes his home in Green Bay.*

DAWN, TOFT POINT NATURAL AREA, MOONLIGHT BAY

PREVIOUS PAGE—WINTER DAYBREAK, CAVE POINT

TREES IN THE MIST, CAVE POINT

*I guess what continues to fascinate me about this place—
and I'm speaking now as a writer who lives here—is that
after many books and all the years of living in it, I'm still
not able to really define the place. Water defines some of it,
but not all. The light here is different because of the water
that surrounds everything, but that's not all of it either.*

*There is a spiritual aspect to the landscape.
When you try to write what Door County is about,
it's about something as elusive as that: spirit.*

*That is the mystery which is all-compelling.
If anything holds me here, and struggles to make
its presence felt in light of man's continued efforts
to destroy it for the sake of greed, it would be spirit.*

—from *Meditations on a Small Lake*
by Norbert Blei

SHOWY LADY'S SLIPPER ORCHIDS, NEAR THE RIDGES SANCTUARY

...it's what the Ridges has done to provide a number of habitats and create this diversity that is fairly unique... it's a living environment of things that few people have experienced. We get people from, literally, all over the world that do come here... just to see what it's like— this natural laboratory that has been created over time.

—Paul Regnier,
Chief Naturalist/Administrator, The Ridges Sanctuary

FOOTBRIDGE OVER SWALE, THE RIDGES SANCTUARY

WINTER TWILIGHT, SHERWOOD POINT LIGHTHOUSE

October 10, 1883:
This Light was lit for the first time October 10th 1883
By Henry Stanley, The Principle Keeper.
J. B. Watson the Commander of the U. S. Navy
Transferd me to this Station from Eagle Bluff Light Station
which I kept for fifteen years.

—first journal entry, by the first keeper,
Henry Stanley, Sherwood Point Lighthouse

ICED OVER CEDARS, CAVE POINT

FISH TUG, "MISS JUDY", JACKSON HARBOR, WASHINGTON ISLAND

A southerly, will it do what we need done
Move an ice flow from here to St. Martin's
I'll owe my catch to the wind
And thank God as I pull my nets in
If it blows us free and lets us sail again

Now there's good times and bad
But we'll get through with the law of averages
Life goes up and down
Like the waves we sail upon
It's a way of life and it's in the blood

The passage that leads us to the lake
Four hours to the nets is what it takes
So drink the coffee strong and black
And spend time thinking back
To a day of old and another catch...

Evening, with the compass set for land
Venus warms the heart but cold still are the hands
Full-bellied seagulls as happy friends
Jackson Harbor is straight ahead
Fishtug welcome, welcome home

—lyrics from *"Fishermen's Song"* by Washington Island musician and songwriter, Julian Hagen; from the album, *Always Be There*

LOWER RANGE LIGHT, THE RIDGES SANCTUARY

Cave Point, Moonlight Bay, Gravel Island, Death's Door—
Those were names that meant something to the sailors.
Could they avoid the shoals and find the range lights of Baileys Harbor,
or would another wife tread solemnly on a rooftop widow's walk
looking for a ship that would never return?

—from *Journeys to Door County*, text by Mike Link;
reprinted with permission from Voyager Press, Stillwater, MN 55082. 1-800-888-9653

LIGHTHOUSE POINT, BAILEYS HARBOR

St. Michael's Chapel

ST MICHAEL'S CHAPEL, WASHINGTON ISLAND

PREVIOUS PAGE—ARCTIC PRIMROSE, THE RIDGES SANCTUARY

Approximately 30 years ago,
my parents bought the Klyen brothers' property
which included the Klyen General Store...
We were one of the few Catholic families
on the Island at that point...

The Catholic community had been meeting
at the American Legion Hall. It was suggested
that what had been the general store
be made into a Catholic chapel.
My parents certainly went along with that.
All furniture and furnishings were donated
by various islanders, not necessarily Catholic.

The chapel was opened to the community...
We've had christenings and we've had weddings...
Our daughter was married in the chapel...

—John Lehman, 50-year summer resident of Washington Island
and owner of St. Michael's Chapel

APPLE BLOSSOMS AND GATE, CHURCH OF THE ATONEMENT, FISH CREEK

ICEBOUND TUGS, STURGEON BAY

ICE SHOVES, SHOEMAKER POINT, BAY OF GREEN BAY

We've seen some wonderful storms out here...
It's interesting, these big black clouds,
as they come up from the west
and head on toward the east...
they get over the lake
and they just kind of pile up—
they really don't know what to do
when they get over the atmosphere of the lake...
then they roll. It's pretty exciting.

—Rosemary Janda, who with husband Louis,
were summertime caretakers at Cana Island Lighthouse from 1977 to 1995

WINTER DAWN, CANA ISLAND LIGHTHOUSE

DAYBREAK OVER HOE ISLAND, SAWYER HARBOR

...it's a life-changing experience
[living on Hoe Island], it has been for me.
You get closer to nature, you're right in it—
the water, the bugs, the birds.
Suddenly you notice things you didn't notice before...
Everything is more interesting to you...
You're just closer to nature.
It almost seems like you're closer to the way
you're really supposed to be.

—Fred Wittig,
poet and sole resident of Hoe Island

ICE COVERED BOAT HOIST WITH CRESCENT MOON, GILLS ROCK

I remember one time, in our small boat,
that was in the thirties, we spent four nights...
off the East Channel— we got caught in an ice storm.

Another time, we were caught in Europe Bay
and there we stayed out overnight.
We couldn't get out of there because of the ice floe.
That was kind of interesting because, in today's world,
they know back home where you are every minute.
but of course, we had no communications at that time...

—Arnie Richter, native Washington Islander
and owner of Washington Island Ferry Line

DAWN SKIES REFLECTED IN ICE, NEAR CANA ISLAND

When mom and dad first met, mom and a couple
of girlfriends had been invited out to the Coast Guard station.
My dad was on duty in, what was then, the lookout building.
He spotted mom and asked his buddy to arrange a date.

On the following Sunday, their first date,
they walked out to the fog signal [north pierhead light]
which, in those days was fired by a coal furnace.
My dad brought a bag of marshmallows and they sat
there roasting marshmallows in that furnace.
Every time I go on that pier, I think,
'mom and dad's first date... and look what happened.'

—Emeryl Trabert, born and raised in Sturgeon Bay,
speaking about her family roots in Door County

NORTH PIERHEAD LIGHT, STURGEON BAY SHIP CANAL

MICHIGAN STREET BRIDGE, STURGEON BAY

You have the bands playing, the National Anthem starts off,
the speeches talking about the great work that our crew does—
and they do a great job! The sponsor cracking the bottle,
and the ship moving down the ways— at only seven knots,
but it makes a big splash. And the Anchors Away plays...
the band, the music, the tears in the eyes of the gals.
It is a very moving experience and one you obviously never get tired of.

—Ellsworth Peterson, speaking as president of Peterson Builders, Inc.
in reference to the launching of U.S. Navy ships from the Peterson Dock

SHIP UNDER CONSTRUCTION, PALMER JOHNSON SHIP BUILDERS, STURGEON BAY

CHAPEL AT BIRTHPLACE OF THE NORBERTINE FATHERS, NAMUR

TRUE FORGET-ME-NOTS AND TREE TRUNK, PENINSULA STATE PARK

FISH TUG, "SOUTHWESTER," BAILEYS HARBOR

I started in fishing when I was eight.
We fished pond nets in the fall for herring.
Older men would dress and wash the
herring and us kids would salt them,
and put them into 130 pound packages.

They say fish is brain food… but I don't know.
I've eaten an awful lot of it…

—The late Spencer Nelson (1904–1994) Washington Island commercial fisherman (Spoken with a twinkle in his eye) From *Over and Back: A Picture History of Transportation to Washington Island* by Dick Purinton

FISH BOXES, BUOYS AND TUG; JACKSON HARBOR, WASHINGTON ISLAND

"PIED PIPER" IN FARM FIELD, NEAR VALMY

Farming as a life certainly has its challenges. But I think that when you grow up on a farm, you have more of a direct connection to how your food is produced. You have more of a respect for the people that produce the food and the clothing that you wear. You don't take it for granted as much as maybe somebody who's not been exposed to a farming situation.

—Richard Weidman, Superintendent,
Agricultural Experimental Station, Sturgeon Bay

CHURCH OF THE ATONEMENT, FISH CREEK

AUTUMN WOODS AND STONE FENCE, NEAR HORSESHOE BAY

That mystique is so difficult
to describe but it has to do
with the ancient Door County
which goes back to the time
of Native American People...
plus the Europeans
that came here 150 years ago...
and while they were clearing fields,
created these beautiful stone walls
that are still to be seen everywhere.

All of that... adds up to
creating this sense of history
which is a part of my music.

—Dan Meunier,
Door County composer-pianist

AUTUMN SHORE, PENINSULA STATE PARK

It's very satisfying, living in the park,
and the most satisfying...
is anticipating the next season...

The springs up here are probably
my second favorite time of the year...
but living in the park during the fall
is probably the best time of all—
when you've got a good mix
of good weather, wonderful color...
you really feel like you're privileged to be here.

—Tom Blackwood, Superintendent
Peninsula State Park, Fish Creek

PITCHER'S THISTLE (THREATENED SPECIES) WHITEFISH DUNES STATE PARK

We just have what is required by an artist.
If I was stuck under the L-train tracks down in Chicago,
it would be a completely different story.
Then I would probably be painting nonobjective,
abstract things that nobody would be able to recognize.
But, when you are saturated with beauty all around you,
well, you can't paint any other way.

—Gerhard Miller, *"Dean of Door County Artists"* and
co-owner with wife, Ruth, of the Gerhard Miller Gallery

DAYBREAK, CAVE POINT

MOONRISE, NEWPORT BAY   PREVIOUS PAGE—SUGAR MAPLE AND SPLIT RAIL FENCE, NEAR SISTER BAY

DUSK OVER EAGLE BLUFF AND HORSESHOE ISLAND

After seventeen years, I returned
[to Door County] with my children...
I've never had this happen before,
but I stepped out of the car at Evergreen Beach...
the minute my foot touched the ground
I looked out over Horseshoe Island
and the bluff, and I thought,
'After all this "who struck John" in my life,
I'm home!' It was like I was the only person
on the peninsula at that point...

That weekend I started looking for property to buy.

—Eleanor McCullin who, in 1986 pulled up stakes
rooted in the East Coast and started life anew in Door County.

SUNSET REFLECTIONS AND SAILBOATS, STURGEON BAY

E. EUGENE HELGESON JR. MEMORIAL LIGHT, ANDERSON DOCK, EPHRAIM

The niceness of Door County... is, well,
the friendliness of the people, the beautiful sunsets,
the walks on the beach when I'm on Washington Island,
crossing the water on the ferry—that's nice,
that's very nice. But I guess maybe it's the people mostly...
You can't enjoy being in a place unless you enjoy the people—
and I have enjoyed the people here.

—Dolores Allen, radio personality,
WDOR, Sturgeon Bay

PIN CHERRY AND MAPLES SILHOUETTED AT SUNSET, NEWPORT STATE PARK

SUGAR MAPLE AND PIN CHERRY, NEWPORT STATE PARK

We are a group of park visitors
who have one thing in common:
we love Newport State Park. Some of us
live here in Door County all year 'round,
while others have visited the park just once
but liked what they saw... We all know that
Newport's wilderness is special and unique.
Not many parks are as pristine and unspoiled
as Newport, and we want the park to remain
as natural in the years to come as it is today.

—Statement by the Newport Wilderness Society,
the official friend's group of Newport State Park

TANNENBAUM'S SISTER BAY

WINTER TWILIGHT, EPHRAIM

VALHOF, VIKING TEMPLE OF VALOR, NEAR EGG HARBOR

The Valhof is a reproduction of a Viking temple as it used to be at the farm sites... I created the Viking temple because there were none in existence (in Door County) and the Vikings themselves were magnificent woodworkers...

It takes a long time of studying to get the essence of what they are trying to represent. So, another reason for me to reproduce the Viking temple was to try to understand exactly how they carved and how they designed. There's an underlying current of meaning in everything that they did. And that current of meaning must be understood before the carving can be executed.

—Greg Urban, Door County woodworker and creator of the Valhof, Viking Temple of Valor

GAZEBO AND AUTUMN MAPLES, GRIFFIN INN, ELLISON BAY

We bought the farm in '55. Emery liked Appaloosas—
they were beautiful... He taught young people
about raising and taking care of horses...

This one young girl would come up almost every summer.
She loved horses and she fell in love with Emery because
he loved horses. They talked horses, horses, horses...
Then she bought that Appaloosa.

Years later we were invited to her wedding.
The Appaloosa was the ring bearer.
And do you know that horse remembered Emery?
He whinnied when Emery walked up to him.

—Irene Oldenburg speaking of her late husband,
Emery "Dynamite" Oldenburg, Door County's "first and last cowboy"

AUTUMN DAYBREAK, NORTH END KANGAROO LAKE

OLDENBURG'S HORSE BARN, NEAR BAILEYS HARBOR

GUS KLENKE GARAGE, ELLISON BAY

DOORFODILS (DAFFODILS UNIQUELY HYBRIDIZED FOR DOOR COUNTY) FISH CREEK

STURGEON BAY SHIP CANAL LIGHTHOUSE AND COAST GUARD STATION

The October, 1880 Great Alpena Blow
was the worst gale in Door County history...

The lighthouse keeper on Cana Island,
William Sanderson, recorded that waves
were going over the lighthouse keeper's house,
had crashed down the door to the kitchen
and were sweeping up inside the
kitchen. The door to the lighthouse had
given way under the waves which were
going up 10 feet inside the lighthouse.

The lighthouse lamp had been put out
by 'sea-spray,' as he put it. He and an assistant,
who was actually just a visitor visiting for the day,
were able to relight the lamp and keep it going.

—P. J. Creviere Jr.,
expert scuba diver and historian

KEEPER'S CAP, GLASSES AND LOG BOOK, EAGLE BLUFF LIGHTHOUSE

CHERRY BLOSSOMS AND BARN, NEAR EGG HARBOR

PREVIOUS PAGE—CLOUDS AND WAVES, BAILEYS HARBOR

SNOWBOUND ANDERSON DOCK, EAGLE HARBOR, EPHRAIM

. . . Windance,

prove what I have always known:

I am a creature of cold clear water and lake wind

not made for dry land, for endless plowing of tired dirt,

tangled mother roots, unshakable stone foundation.

I am wave and pulse, a lover-God's laughter,

formed to skim on water, tip

unafraid to meet wild sea.

Becalmed in hot sun on a lake of glass

I wait to twirl with the shift of wind . . .

I will escape to catch a wind dance that never ceases

and sail eyes-open through eternity.

—excerpt from the poem "Windance," by Door County poet Lauren Mittermann; from her book of poetry, *Different Paths*

SAILING ON GREEN BAY, NEAR PENINSULA STATE PARK

BARN ART AND STONE BARN, WASHINGTON ISLAND FARM MUSEUM

FORESTVILLE FEED AND GRAIN

FISH TUG, "BETTY," SAND BAY

EAGLE BLUFF LIGHTHOUSE, PENINSULA STATE PARK

April 8, 1922:
The Hanson boy drowned
in the Chanel near Fish Creek.
I tried my best to save him.
Had to walk to Fish Creek for help.
The telephone was out of order.

April 10, 1922:
Keeper lit light in tower tonight
for a small boat going to Chambers Island
to get Sam Hanson...
to attend his boy's funeral.

—Lighthouse journal entries by Peter Coughlin,
the last keeper at Eagle Bluff Lighthouse, 1918–1926

...there's quite a cultural influence here.
Over the years, Door County has been known
for attracting musicians, artists—you name it...
then also the beauty of the place.
So you have the environmental quality...
mixed with the cultural,
but with a little quieter pace
than you have in the large city areas.

—Mitchell Mackey, past president,
Door County Historical Society

WHITE LACE INN, STURGEON BAY

BELGIAN FARMHOUSE, NEAR MAPLEWOOD

PREVIOUS PAGE—CHERRIES IN BUCKETS, CHERRY ORCHARD, NEAR FISH CREEK

Je'm foot sa	*I Don't Care*
Je'm foot sa	*I don't care*
J'a de canada	*I have potatoes*
J'a di pomme de terre	*I have apples from the ground*
E J'a de pomme de terre	*And I have apples from the ground*
Je'm foot sa j'a de canada	*I don't care, I have potatoes*
J'a de pomme de terre	*I have apples from the ground*
Pau passie min ivierr	*To pass the winter*
(Walloon ditty)	*(English translation)*

—from *Phonetic Walloon for Belgian Americans*
by Door County native, farm wife and writer, Josephine LeGrave Wautlet
(Walloon is the native language of the Belgian Americans who settled in southern Door County and the surrounding area, comprising the largest Belgian settlement in the United States.)

FERRY, "ROBERT NOBLE" AND FERRY LINE TRUCK, DETROIT HARBOR, WASHINGTON ISLAND

CHRISTENING BLESSING

O Lord our God, regard with favor the men who shall man this boat.
Watch over their bodies and souls and cause them to show
forth a life of dedication to all who depend on them.

May all who ride upon the EYRARBAKKI find time between
the two shores to reflect upon the great beauty around us
and do all in their power to maintain it.

May the EYRARBAKKI itself, O Lord, sail safely over the waves
at all times. May it always be used to bring joy into the lives
of all who ride upon her. May it always be used as an instrument
of mercy and a carrier of all things needed for life... AMEN

—From the blessing of the EYRARBAKKI-1970 by Reverend Chester C. Nerenhausen, then Pastor of Trinity Lutheran Church, Washington Island

CUPOLA HOUSE, EGG HARBOR

APPLE BLOSSOMS, NEAR EGG HARBOR

DAYBREAK, TOFT POINT, MOONLIGHT BAY

MISTY SUNRISE THRU EVERGREENS, THE RIDGES SANCTUARY

One of the main reasons we came to Door County is that we love the boreal forests which stretch along the Lake Michigan shoreline from the Mink River to the Ridges Sanctuary. This is the area where one can get the feeling of being in a true wilderness area. It is one of the most valuable aspects of Door County... very precious and needs to be preserved.

—Warren Dewalt,
President of the Newport Wilderness Society

DWARF LAKE IRIS (THREATENED SPECIES) THE RIDGES SANCTUARY

It seems as if Mother Nature was not satisfied with giving Door County the largest number of native orchids, but also she gave this peninsula county the largest number of other rare plants that are to be found in Wisconsin. Around Decoration Day, the area resembles a gigantic flower garden with a riot of color…

Many of our large cities have spent millions of dollars to reproduce what Mother Nature has given Door County free of charge…

This area not only belongs to Door County but it also belongs to the people of Wisconsin, and above all it belongs to future generations.

—Dr. Albert Fuller whose efforts led the way in establishing The Ridges Sanctuary in 1937: from the *Door County Advocate*; February 19, 1937

SUNRISE, AHNAPEE RIVER, NEAR FORESTVILLE

Rarely does Nature fail to produce some thrilling experiences
for those who take to the out-of-doors, are eager to learn,
and are willing to be patient and observant.
Door County, rich in native plants and animals
is an ideal classroom for such experiences.
People who learn to understand and enjoy our natural resources
will not be satisfied unless they can repeat these experiences
year after year. And if many, many people develop this noble attitude,
our beautiful county will stand a chance of remaining beautiful—
and perhaps even improving its natural condition.

—from *Once Around the Sun*,
by Roy Lukes, Door County naturalist and author

TENNISON BAY, PENINSULA STATE PARK

We are glad that Simon Kahquados has come back to Door County for his final rest, for this was the place he loved best of all. Here he played as a boy, here he hunted as a man, and here his ancestors had dwelt for centuries. They 'loved these rocks and rills, these woods and templed hills' just as we do...

—Hjalmar R. Holand, then president of the Door County Historical Society, speaking at the burial of Simon Kahquados, Head Chief of the Potawatomi Indians, at Peninsula State Park, Memorial Day, 1931

AUTUMN SUGAR MAPLE, NEAR STURGEON BAY

SUNRISE, MOONLIGHT BAY

People long to see sunsets
and they'll drive hundreds of miles
to take in sunsets over our water…
I really think that they're missing
the best part of the day in the sunrise.

I appreciate that time, both for its beauty
and as a time when I'm on the water, and
I can talk to my God and he understands me.
That's a very precious time.

—Jeff Weborg, fourth generation
Door County commercial fisherman

YELLOW LADY'S SLIPPER ORCHID, THE RIDGES SANCTUARY

After I am gone, my restrictions live on.
I do have the pleasant thought that the
yellow lady's slippers, trillium, the red fox,
the visiting cranes, dogwood, buffalo berry,
princess pine and blackberries will stay around.

—Door County land owner, Ruth Neuman,
upon assigning a perpetual conservation easement to her property

WEATHERED BARN, NEAR MAPLE GROVE

WINTER DAWN, LAKE MICHIGAN PREVIOUS PAGE—SUNRISE, HISTORIC ROWLEY'S BAY PIER

...I pulled a couple of boards from the scow and putting these on the ice endeavored to pull myself toward the island that I had left the Wednesday before. This was only partly successful, however, and I broke or fell through again, one time going clean down...

I managed to get back to the surface again through the hole I had fallen, altho' it proved to be a terrible job to do this. I then abandoned the boards and began to break the ice where it was not strong enough to hold me, and pulled myself over it where it was. After a terrific struggle I at last reached the ice banks a little south of the entrance to Detroit Harbor on the Island of that name. But my troubles were not over yet. I was so covered with ice that my clothes weighted me down and I could not get over the banks...

—Robert Noble describing his 1864 ordeal which earned him the nickname, *"Iron Man of the Door,"* from an interview in the February 28, 1903 *Door County Advocate*

BUSH AND SNOWDRIFTS, CANA ISLAND

"YANKEE MAYFLOWER", WASHINGTON HARBOR, WASHINGTON ISLAND

A masterpiece, by a master's hand
Is Washington Harbor indeed.
In the sign of luck—with a horseshoe shape
With graceful beauty decreed...

This work of eternal rippling effect
As the waters lift and subside
Makes the uniform smoothness of every stone
With a rubbing of side against side.

The water will rise and the stones will rub
With a furious storm from the east,
It will push, it will swell, with fullness and lift
Like the chest of a brutal beast.

But then if you look at the other extreme
When the water is placid and calm
with sunshine and shade reflecting the clouds
It's like holding the world in your palm...

—excerpt from the poem, "Washington Harbor" by Jack E. Jacobsen
from *Island Life*, a volume of poetry about Washington Island.

SUNRISE, SCHOOLHOUSE BEACH, WASHINGTON ISLAND

PAINTED CUP AND BLACK-EYED SUSAN, TOFT POINT NATURAL AREA

RED BARN AND STORM CLOUDS, NEAR EGG HARBOR

It's hard to get old in Door County...
there's always something...
particularly for a rural area,
the range of experience is very good...

And finally, there's the beauty...
maybe there's a kind of subliminal quality
to beauty too, that it does become part
and parcel of one's self.

—Hal Grutzmacher, deceased former owner,
Passtimes Books and Occasions, Sister Bay

"DIVIDED HIGHWAY," POTAWATOMI STATE PARK

BACKYARD OUTHOUSE, NEAR PENINSULA CENTER

AUTUMN SUGAR MAPLE, NEAR THE CLEARING

I spend a lot of time walking in the woods
and walking in places that are beautiful—
just simply to absorb the solitude and to
absorb shape, to absorb color and that sense
of light that is really unique in Door County.
There's a sense of spirituality for me
that I feel living here and it's grown
as I've been here longer...

—Bonnie Oehlert Smith,
artist and director of the Miller Art Center

ICICLES ON WHITE CEDAR, CAVE POINT

I think the winters in Door County are terrific.
They're mild, we get our snow...
you can cross-country ski...
for those of us that live here...
we feel that winter is the slow-down, quiet time.

—Donald Buchholz, resident manager,
The Clearing, Ellison Bay

WINTER DAYBREAK, CAVE POINT

WHITE CEDARS AND ROCKY SHORE, ROCK ISLAND

LILY PADS AND SEDGES, MINK RIVER ESTUARY

SUGAR MAPLE AND FENCE ROW, NEAR CLARK LAKE

I enjoy my work.

If I didn't enjoy my work,

I wouldn't be at it…

That's part of my lifestyle,

that's my individuality.

I love it…

—Ed "Pudge" DeGraff, artisan and co-owner with fellow artisan and wife, Mary, of DeGraff Woodcarving Studio, Sturgeon Bay

SUNRISE ALONG AHNAPEE STATE TRAIL, NEAR FORESTVILLE

LONE SAILBOAT AT DUSK, FISH CREEK

WINTER SUNRISE, WHITEFISH DUNES STATE PARK

It is significant that Door County
has 13 designated natural areas...
those areas will be protected forever...
It's another indication... that Door County
certainly is a unique area ecologically.

—Carl Scholz, natural history expert and
co-owner of The Farm, Sturgeon Bay

DAYBREAK ON NEWPORT BAY

Door County captured my interest at an early age.
It lured me away from my Peninsula State Park campsite
and hid me in a cedar forest, much to the dismay of
park rangers searching for this lost seven-year old.
The peninsula hasn't lost its grip.

Today, the lakeshore waves that pound Door County crest beneath my sea kayak, and the peninsula's quaint country roads disappear beneath the tires of my touring bike. Its forests still shelter my hiking boots from a world of rapid transit while its beautiful beaches provide a welcome pillow of sand on a lazy summer day.

—from *Exploring Door County* by Craig Charles; copyright 1990 by Craig Charles; reprinted by permission of NorthWord Press, Inc.

Acknowledgements

The process of nurturing this book from conception to completion has been a long one—complete with trials and tribulations as well as triumphs and jubilations. I will forever be appreciative of the unwavering love and support given throughout, by my family and friends.

Thank you Ellie, for introducing me to the wonder of Door County and for sharing your contagious enthusiasm for this unique Great Lakes peninsula.

Thank you Nancy Small, for giving me my first glimpse of what would eventually become a special place of solace, The Ridges Sanctuary.

I wish to thank the crew at the Door County Chamber of Commerce, both past and present, for their recognition and encouragement of my photography in Door County.

My sincere gratitude to both Evelyn Shapiro and Becky Mead. With unbridled enthusiasm and great artistic vision, their initial involvement shaped the book's design, giving it a sense of order and grace.

To the competent and caring staff at Trails Media Group: thank you for sharing my vision and supporting my ideas. Your involvement and commitment to this project have transformed a dream into reality. A very special thank you to Nancy Mead for initiating the process.

I am indebted to Tom Davis for contributing both his valuable time and his prodigious talent to write the introduction. His insightful prologue gives cohesiveness to the varied images and passages placing them into a meaningful context.

WILD GERANIUM WITH DEW, NEAR FORESTVILLE

A very special thank you to all of the people who openly shared their stories, their thoughts and their feelings–these comprised the essence of the quotations which are such an integral part of the book. Research for these passages was greatly aided by many people who readily extended a helping hand. My sincere appreciation to Dick Purinton, Lucy Roske, Kathleen Regnier, Steve Karges, Peg Foster and the respective staffs at the Door County Maritime Museum, the Door County Library and the Door County Advocate.

I am especially grateful to Mike and Sue McFadzen, Mary Pappas, and Rick Martens of Trails & Tales who produced the magnificent audio tape, *Door County Tapestry*. Through their generosity and invaluable assistance, this tape and related interviews served as the source for numerous quotations.

And finally, I am particularly thankful to people like Jens Jensen, Emma Toft, Albert Fuller and many others, who years ago had the wisdom, foresight and courage to dedicate their efforts to the preservation of Door County's beautiful and fragile natural areas. The same gratitude is extended to all those who have since picked up the torch and continue on with this important and worthy cause.

Daryl R. Beers

QUOTATIONS INDEX

** Quotations from interviews by Trails & Tales (1860 Preble Ave., Green Bay, WI 54302, Ph 920-437-0637) for production of the audio tape,* Door County Tapestry.